RESTORE YOUR MARRIAGE

YOUR MARRIAGE CAN BE REPAIRED AND YOU CAN FEEL NEW LOVE

OLAJUMOKE O. AKINTOLA

ISBN: 9798351341811

DEDICATION

This book is dedicated to my Dad Chief Akintola Sunday I. and to my students, even those who have not discovered my contents.

CONTENTS

Restore Your Marriage

Your marriage can be repaired, and you can feel new love.

Chapter 1:
Being Married

Synopsis

In this chapter, I'll discuss some of the numerous commitments and adjustments that marriage brings to your life.

- Be careful when choosing a companion.
- Be aware of your own needs as well as those of others.
- You should be able to live, love, and share.
- Focus More On Listening Than Speaking
- Prepare yourself for some changes and challenges.

The Fundamentals

Every single one of us leads one of two different types of lives: the single life or the married life. Everyone needs to comprehend the many contrasts between these two lives because if you don't, you'll mistakenly think that they are the same, and then things will get tense. Things might get quite challenging for your marriage, especially if you don't adapt to married life and keep doing the same things you did when you were single. The conversation that follows will outline the things you should be aware of before committing to a married life.

Be careful when choosing a companion.

Finding the ideal companion to spend the rest of your life with is the first and most crucial step. Though it might sometimes be quite important, doing something can also be extremely simple. You should take your time getting to know each other before getting married in either situation. This will give you a better idea of how drastically different your personalities are from one another and how many adjustments you will need to make to the relationship in order to survive. You can trust your instincts and move toward a healthier and stronger married relationship if you can see that you two are synchronizing with one another well and that there aren't many differences arising during your relationship. However, if you are having trouble changing that person's attitude, you may want to consider other options. If you feel that everything will be okay once you get married, things can only grow worse, believe me when I say that nothing will be okay.

Be aware of your own needs as well as those of others.

This is a crucial factor that aids in your decision-making process when selecting a partner. Prior to trying to find someone like you, you should first strive to get to know yourself well, including your strengths, weaknesses, personality traits, and similar things. Knowing oneself entails continually presenting oneself to others in the manner that you would like to be treated. The wrong approach to go about developing a relationship is to frequently witness someone lie or make up things. Ask basic questions about beliefs and other such topics to get to know the other person thoroughly. You can gain a deeper grasp of that person's mindset and any potential issues with that attitude by asking them these straightforward questions.

You should be able to live, love, and share

When a new relationship is beginning, it's important to allow the other person enough time to get to know you. This time should not only entail meeting up for dinner and other social activities; you also need to demonstrate a lot of other things to the other person. You can never anticipate receiving affection and care later in life if it isn't present in those formative years. These are highly fundamental demands in a relationship, and their absence indicates that the other person is either not prepared for a relationship or is not mentally stable to be with you.

Focus More On Listening Than Speaking

Another critical component of relationships is listening, and this is especially true early on. You must pay attention to the other person in order to understand how they see the world and how they want to live their lives. People often speak more than they listen, but this is not how it should be. After stating your case clearly the first time, pay close attention to what the other person is saying and attempt to understand what they are trying to convey to you through their thoughts and conversations.

Prepare yourself for some changes and challenges.

It is common knowledge that if you try to start a new relationship, there will be challenges and difficulties. However, if you start to panic about these challenges, things will only grow worse. You will learn how accepting the other person is of you by way of these minor issues and discrepancies. In these circumstances, you must maintain your composure and try to avoid giving the impression that you are willing to sacrifice anything for the relationship. Instead, if necessary, make small adjustments to give the impression that you are making an effort to make things work. If the other person is completely rattled by these issues, you should consider an alternative option and look for a better person.

Chapter 2:
Making Your Relationship Stronger

Synopsis

I'll share some crucial information with you in this chapter that can strengthen and improve your connection.

- Relating to each other
- Show your relationship some tenderness
- Eliminate any communication gaps.
- Time is right for your connection.
- Confidence

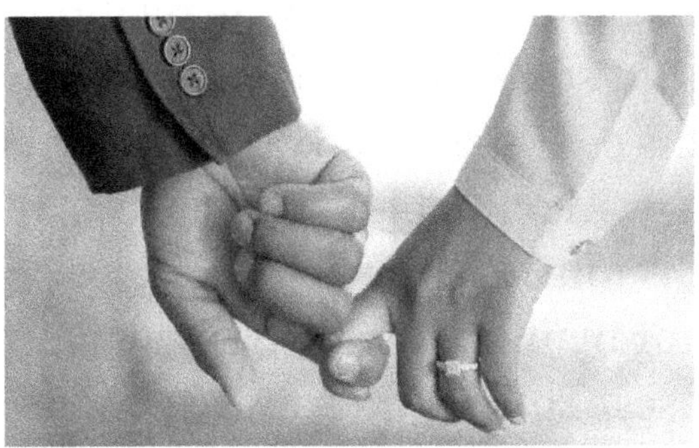

Enhancing It's Stability

You have already learnt all the crucial information that you need to know before starting any relationship, but now we'll take it a step further and talk about some crucial information that you should know after starting a relationship. It's simple to enter into a relationship or make a commitment, but it's much harder to keep it going. If you don't understand the fundamental elements needed to make a relationship work, you risk ending it or losing yourself in its complications. The need to look out for one another and make an effort to improve your relationship is especially beneficial in husband-wife relationships.

Relating to each other

The key to a successful husband-wife relationship is responsibility, but some individuals frequently misinterpret this concept, believing that the husband is solely accountable for all aspects of the marriage. This is untrue because equal responsibility for maintaining the relationship lies with both spouses. Things will start to go wrong if any of them believes they are not at fault. Both partners have distinct kinds of duties. While the husband must take care of everything, the wife's duty is more supporting. Small misunderstandings will inevitably happen, but if you are accountable enough to acknowledge your error, these misunderstandings will actually strengthen your relationship.

Show your relationship some tenderness

We always love to get care, and this is just part of being human. This is valid for relationships between husbands and wives since your bond will become stronger the more you care for one another. Care is a two-way street; if one spouse isn't taking care of the other, the other partner won't bother to take care of the other.

There are some very minor things involved in care, but it is not something that is extremely difficult or precise that you cannot perform. For instance, even a simple phone call to your wife to ask how she is doing and to reassure her that you would always remember her would be a really thoughtful gesture on her part.

Similar to this, if you're a wife, all it takes to reassure your spouse that you love him is a kind smile when he gets home from a long day at work.

Eliminate any communication gaps

Lack of communication is yet another critical aspect that might sour your connection. The cornerstone to successful new relationships is communication. Without it, you won't be able to express to your partner how much you care about them or what sort of attitude you have. Ultimately, if you share less, you'll learn less as well. It takes a lot of speaking and a sincere desire to learn everything you can about someone in order to get to know them well. It is not required that you exclusively inquire about important and significant matters; rather, you can begin with simple and uncomplicated topics of conversation before moving on to more complicated life difficulties.

As you won't be able to get to know the other person well if you speak too much and listen too little, this is also not a very good relationship practice. Clarifying yourself entirely before listening closely to the other person is the greatest method to communicate and get to know them. Your relationship will get stronger as a result of your greater communication, but it will also allow you to reduce misunderstandings more efficiently because anytime something goes wrong in your relationship, you can talk it out in detail and the issue can be properly resolved.

Time is right for your connection

Furthermore, timing is very important, so you must give your relationship enough time. Today's breakups are most commonly caused by people spending less time in relationships. Today's society requires most people to work long hours every day just to get by and maintain their standard of living. However, in the hustle and bustle of daily life, relationships frequently suffer as people prioritize their careers over their personal lives and break up. If you are a husband or wife who works, you should examine your weekly schedule to see how much time you are spending with your partner and family. You will learn from this study how much effort you still have to do on your relationship and how much more time you need to devote to it. You will also learn that you need to break your previous routine and habit of arriving home late. You should occasionally leave the office early to give your relationship a sense of surprise. This modest act will cost you nothing, but it will greatly please your partner and give the impression that you are concerned about them.

CONFIDENCE

A shared sense that you need to cultivate in your relationships is trust, which is still another essential quality. You cannot reasonably expect your partner to trust you if you do not. Being in a relationship with someone you can trust entails more than simply having faith in their loyalty to you; it also includes having confidence in their ability to uphold all of their relationship commitments.

If you put in a little extra effort, all of the aforementioned suggestions can help you build strong, healthy relationships. They are all quite simple to follow in your daily life and do not involve anything particularly complicated. Because stress is always bad for your health, having healthy relationships and avoiding conflict can also improve your physical well-being.

Chapter 3:
Take charge of your marriage and make it more solid

Synopsis

You will learn about every significant factor that can help you have a more stable and successful marriage in this chapter.

- Establish guidelines and adhere to them
- Each other's assistance
- Never let your relationship's romanticism to fade.

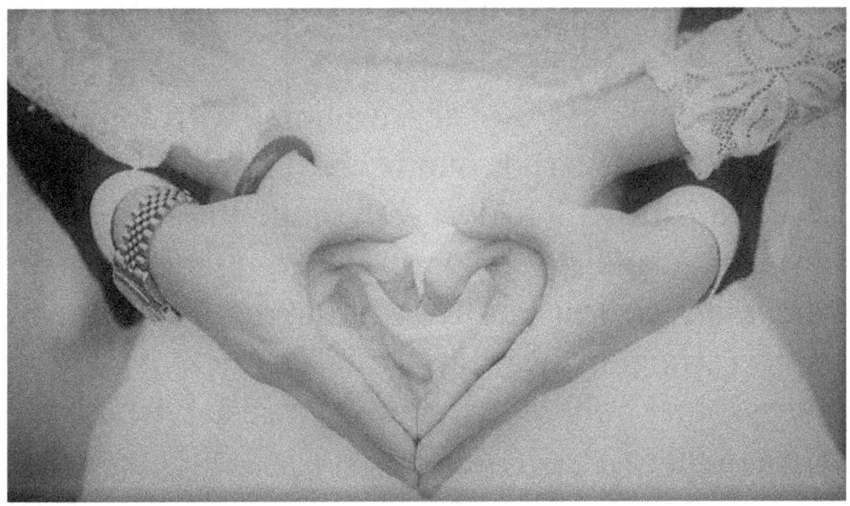

- Stability of finances

Create Stability

Today's marriages frequently experience misunderstandings and breakdowns in communication, and most of the time, this is because the couple has handled their relationship improperly. You must understand that a husband-wife relationship is highly fragile and requires a lot of care and attention from both parties to stay on the right track. The conversation that follows will outline the fundamental requirements you must meet in order to have an all-encompassing marriage that is stronger.

Establish guidelines and adhere to them

It can be challenging to share a home with someone, and when your backgrounds are different, it can be even more difficult to deal with the contrasts that you have managed to incorporate into each other's personalities. You can live without any problems by using a straightforward way. Make sure that you and your partner adhere to the rules you establish for the household.

The tendency of husbands and wives to keep their likes and dislikes a secret is common, yet doing so can make life much easier and simpler Simply thinking that your spouse will know what you want will not result in what you desire, so instead of remaining silent, you may simply tell him what you want him to do. Similar to this, there are a variety of additional straightforward guidelines that, when adhered to, can prevent a great deal of misunderstandings.

Each other's assistance

There are duties that you and your partner must carry out when you share a house. If you are a husband, then you are required to assist your wife in all aspects of everyday domestic duties. This is especially important on weekends because your wife needs time to herself and even the smallest amount of your assistance will make her feel incredibly appreciated.

Similar to this, it is your duty as a wife to give your husband the best level of comfort that you are able to provide. If you give your husband a sweet smile as soon as he enters the house, it will make everything better and give him the impression that his entire day's work has been well spent. However, if you start yelling at him right away, it will start to build tension, and your husband won't be too happy about that.

Never let your relationship's romanticism to fade
Most of the time, your relationship gets predictable and everything becomes known after spending some time with your spouse. It's common for people to add

romance to situations of this predictable type, but this is not the best strategy to use. Instead, you should work to maintain romance throughout your relationship. There are numerous different things that can make your relationship more romantic besides just having sex in bed.

Bringing a straightforward flower is also considered romantic if you are leaving the office and pass a flower shop on the way. This modest, practically free gesture may make your life incredibly romantic and can instill your partner with a very positive impression of you. In order to maintain passion in your relationship, keep doing such gestures.

Stability of finances

Another factor that contributes to long-lasting relationships is having stable finances, which provides you a very secure social position and significantly reduces your stress and daily anxieties. If you are too lazy to change your financial condition, it is not true what some men claim: that their spouses do not support them when they are in difficult financial situations.

There isn't a lady in this world who won't stand with you through tough times if you are passionate about the cause and making an effort to improve your life; nevertheless, issues begin when you give up on improving. Give your best effort at all times so that your partner will support you. Similar to this, a wife should work and support her husband in whatever manner she can if she notices that he is unable to provide for the family's financial needs.

Chapter 4:
Ways to End Differences in Your Marriage

Synopsis

I'm going to share with you some insider suggestions in this chapter that, should you experience any marital difficulties, can help you get over them.

- Be optimistic at all times and take ownership of your actions.
- Happiness without conditions
- Change yourself first if you want your mate to change.
- Your relationship can become more solid and unbreakable with forgiveness.
- In your relationship, spirituality can foster peace and modesty.

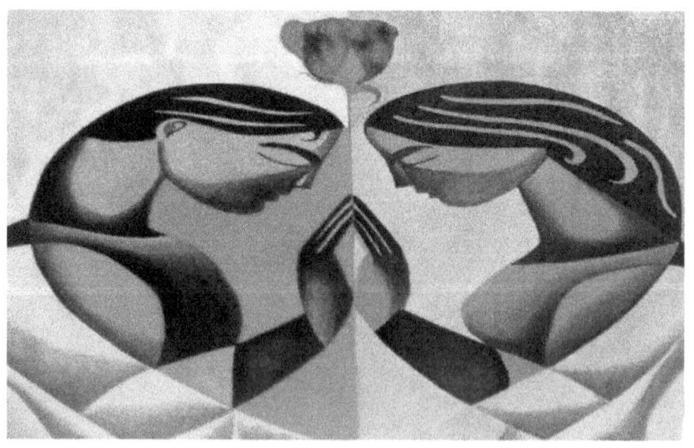

Be Companionable

You have to live a completely different life as a married pair. You have to make a lot of concessions, and you also have to do a lot of things against your better judgment, but everything you do is for the greater good of your future. There is nothing wrong with making a few little concessions to make your future life easier and healthier; however, you should never let your ego get in the way of these decisions. In the discussions mentioned above, I first explained how to choose the ideal mate for you, and then I explained what factors can increase the effectiveness and longevity of your marriage. I'm going to talk to you in this conversation about some steps and approaches you can take if there has been miscommunication or confusion in your relationship.

Be optimistic at all times and take ownership of your actions

It is common knowledge that anytime there is a miscommunication, it is not the fault of one party alone; both parties are equally responsible. Few people are able to accept this fact because everyone begins to assign blame and no one is willing to acknowledge their own shortcomings. You should change your mindset, and you should have the courage to admit when you were wrong and to express your regret. It is simpler for the other person to accept their own fault if you have acknowledged your own error or fault and have admitted responsibility for it. It's important to maintain a positive outlook on your relationship and to never consider ending it; instead, always try to find a workable solution.

Happiness without conditions

Some people believe that specific activities would make them happier, whilst for others, staying home is dull and monotonous. This shouldn't be the case because there are many happy moments to be found in everyday life, even if they are modest and unassuming. It should also make you happy, for instance, when you play games with your children. Nowadays, individuals frequently overlook these little joys in life in favor of waiting for major occasions. This approach strains relationships and makes people forget about the lesser joys in life.

Change yourself first if you want your mate to change

Some people constantly seek to include distinctive elements into their lives, but it can be quite challenging for others to do the same. This is not the proper method to alter someone; instead, you should start by making some modifications that your partner will like. Your partner will be inspired to change when you make those adjustments to your personality because they will understand that you have accepted their opinions and changed yourself, therefore it is now their turn to make the changes you prefer.

Your relationship can become more solid and unbreakable with forgiveness

Life has gotten really difficult recently, as I said above, and there is little time for taking care of one another. There is turmoil and excessive stress everywhere you look as a result of the hectic lifestyle that has also robbed this culture of forgiveness and tolerance. No one is willing to overlook even the smallest error committed by others. If you share that kind of intolerant attitude, you must alter it for the benefit of a bigger good and to strengthen your bond with your partner. Relationships can only be strengthened through forgiveness, and when you forgive your partner's minor transgressions, he or she begins to respect you more. This means that minor disagreements will never end your relationship.

In your relationship, spirituality can foster peace and modesty

There is far too little room in our lives for spirituality, and we live far too materialistically. You don't need to practice a particular religion in order to be spiritual; all you need to do is be extremely honest with yourself about your beliefs and work to make your life run more smoothly by engaging in some mind-calming activities. With the help of these exercises, you can greatly improve your relationship approach by becoming more composed and modest.

Chapter 5:
Preventing breakups

Synopsis

You can use the advice I give you in this chapter to keep your relationships intact.

- Understand the dynamics of both families.
- Give your relationship the time it needs to grow.
- It's crucial to have emotional support.
- Specify issues, then give the other person a chance to speak.
- Always keep your misunderstandings to the point.

Remain Vigorous

Although arguments will inevitably arise in partnerships, you should always try to find a solution. Insofar as they provide you the opportunity to get to know one another better, even little conflicts can strengthen your relationship. The advice that follows can help you stay out of arguments of all kinds and stay together.

Understand the dynamics of both families

In your new connections, there may be a lot of issues, but in order to resolve them, you must comprehend the dynamics of the families involved. It may be necessary to make certain concessions in order to adopt the customs and patterns of both of your families, as there may be many distinct ones. Both parties must actively participate in this situation, and you must adopt a shared understanding in doing so.

Give your relationship the time it needs to grow

Every relationship needs correct timing, but new relationships especially require that you allow them the time they need to develop. Even while everyday requirements might be highly demanding and life can be very busy at times, relationships always require attention and time. The routine that forms over time needs to be broken as well. Your regular existence should always have a little of surprise. You should give each other some time to adjust even if there was a fight or misunderstanding at the moment.

It's crucial to have emotional support

You must recognize the disparities in your lives that separate you in order to provide emotional support. You need to learn to disagree, according to a proverb. It is imperative that you live by this phrase in your daily relationships since it is both extremely true and quite specific. You should encourage your partner in some way as well as thoroughly consider their viewpoint. It's important for you to realize that modifications need to be made on both ends. While letting the other partner complete their part, you should play yours.

Specify issues, then give the other person a chance to speak

Another extremely typical issue is that when a couple has a disagreement, neither partner listens to the other and instead continues to voice their opinions in private. This is the wrong strategy, and it will never help you solve your difficulties. Instead, you should take the approach of doing things clearly the first time, and then beginning to pay attention to your spouse. As a result, you'll be able to hear the other person better and understand what they're saying.

This will also give you a chance to clear your throat. Simply put, you should have excellent listening skills and use them in your relationships.

Always keep your misunderstandings to the point

Another extremely common error that most couples make is that they begin by blaming one another, and once a misunderstanding arises, they continue to bring up everything from the past to further compound the issue. Because it complicates matters and you should always be vigilant about a particular misunderstanding, this should be avoided. Avoid veering off course and attempt to tackle the problem as a whole rather than combining all the previous concerns into one and confuse everyone about the solution.

Chapter 6:
Several General Techniques and Current Trends for Strengthening Your Marriage

Synopsis

I'll give you some more specific and all-encompassing strategies to assist you rebuild your marriage in this chapter.

- Don't be in a rush
- Acknowledge the viewpoint of others
- Progressively develop together
- The secret to a happy marriage is to have faith and confidence in one another

Tips for Everyone

The tactics and recommendations listed above can actually help you save your marriage and turn it into a very powerful tie between two souls if you are married and seeking assistance. There are some additional significant factors that might significantly aid you in finding actual soul mates. The final items that can help you strengthen and maintain your connection are listed below.

Do Not Be Too Desperate

Most people today come from dysfunctional families, and because of this, they can become so desperate to find a family that they sometimes make poor decisions. It is true that you should always seek a better life, but in your quest, you should never lose sight of the fact that your own life is also on the line. A poor decision in a spouse or other such matter can have a disastrous effect on your entire existence. Give it some thought before making a decision.

Acknowledge the viewpoint of others

It might be quite difficult to comprehend another person's point of view on various issues, yet doing so is essential since only by understanding someone on their level can you truly communicate and express your feelings. It's important to try to see things from the other person's perspective and think as they would in order to ensure that you have fully grasped their perspective and mentality. When you start understanding him, you'll be able to employ the methods that are more practical and in line with his attitude and beliefs, which will help you express your own ideas more clearly as well.

Progressively develop together

This is another key aspect of any relationship: individuals constantly assume that their partners will remain the same even after 10, 15, or more years have gone. However, this is the wrong strategy because both people and things change with time, and this is also true of personalities.

You must accept the changes that happen with time and, in fact, you must be happy to see them. Things will grow difficult for the other person if you start to push back against those changes, and he or she will do the same if you do. So, never accept that your partner will change throughout your relationship in order to preserve and strengthen it.

The secret to a happy marriage is to have faith and confidence in one another

A good marriage is built on a foundation of faith and confidence, among other things. Your life can be a bed of flowers if these two conditions are met, but if not, it could be more harder than you had anticipated. Both of these emotions are shared, and if one partner begins to have faith in the other, the other person will respect and have faith in you as well. Husband and wife spying on one another is human nature. Keep trust and confidence as the driving force behind your relationship in order to avoid such circumstances.

The conclusion

I tried to cover practically all of the necessary information in the aforementioned EBook to help you make your marriage work, and I am confident that even if you apply half of what I've mentioned above to your relationship, you won't experience any problems.

Marriage is a difficult stage of life, especially in the beginning because you are linked to someone you barely know and must spend the rest of your life with them. Most individuals worry when they enter this connection because it looks like such a difficult position, but if you can keep your nerves under control and approach the situation with modesty and composure, it might turn out to be a moment in your life that is well worth investing.

Some people find their first years of marriage to be particularly memorable, while others, because of the challenges and complexities they encountered, do not wish to recall their first years of marriage.

If you are wanting to be married, are already married, or even if you are experiencing marital difficulties, you will discover a step-by-step solution in the discussion above. This information about everyone can improve your life.

Because I made an effort to keep things extremely simple for everyone, I am confident that readers of all ages will read and appreciate this EBook. I also hope you will give it positive comments. I anticipate it making a difference in people's lives and demonstrating to me the value of my research.

www.ingramcontent.com/pod-product-compliance
Lightning Source LLC
LaVergne TN
LVHW020534160826
845677LV00015B/4056
9798351341811